Loving God II

by

Ashanti Witherspoon

This is the second edition of Loving God II. The original was published in 1998, while I was still incarcerated in the Louisiana State Penitentiary, at Angola, Louisiana. This second edition is the same as the original printing with the exception of the publisher and the change in a few of the words.

Published by

The Society of Servant Leaders, Inc.
P.O. Box 902
Baton Rouge, Louisiana 70821

About This Book

Loving God II is the second collection of poems in a series of books written by me while I was serving a seventy-five year sentence in the Louisiana State Penitentiary in Angola, Louisiana. Each morning I wrote a letter, poem, prose to God. The writings spanned for over a decade.

It is dedicated to everyone who has learned how to listen to the "still small voice in their heart."

Table of Contents

A Time For Rest

God did not rest
Until His work was done
The perfection
Of its completion
Brought forth Light.

Light
The power of His Thought
The power of His World
The power of His Love.

Rest did not come
Until all was done
That could be done
In the newness of Life.

April 16, 1998

As I opened my eyes

As I open my eyes this morning
I give thanks to the Creator
that another day has dawned
that will allow me
to do more
of what He has destined
for me to do.

The union
the oneness
the complete communion
with
The Creator
of all things
through the Power
of The Spirit
magnifies my awareness
of the plan that I have to fulfill.

And as I rise and step forth
to face the challenges of the week
I will know that each step
and every thought
is ordained by God
and I shall succeed.

September 10, 1998

Whispers

The whispers from God's Heart
Gave sound
To the still, small voice
That resounded
In my heart.

The whispers from God's Heart
Shape the universe
In accordance with the power
That rises
In everyone's heart.

The whispers from God's Heart
Give life
And meaning
To everything.

January 30, 1998

Thanking God

The greatest blessing
in the world
is when one
can thank God
for the things
He's yet to give.

November 25, 1998

Watching God

Watching God
as He shows me His Love
is fascinating and a wonderful experience
to live through.

His movements
are sometimes overlooked
because they come in many shapes
and many forms.

We walk
in and out of His blessings
so many times during the day
we often don't realize
that a miracle has taken place.

God is like that.

His miracles never cease.
His blessings are continuous.
And, often, we are too blind to see.

July 30, 1998

Witnessing

Witnessing God's goodness
in everything around us
causes us to realize
that God is us
in action
in everything.

Not to realize that
will cause one to experience
the detachment
from all that is real
and
all that is spiritual.

The universality of all things
is found in the teachings of Jesus
the disciples
the apostles
and
all of the sages and saints.
It is also found
in the heart
of those who know God.
It is those individuals who can witness
to the goodness of God's omniscience.

February 3, 1998

In Victory

In victory
God works through those
who willingly allow Him
to work through them
in the work they perform in life.

God seeks victory
through willing vessels
who are willing to recognize
the power of Him
which is them.

God seeks to link
the power of all creation
through all of creation
and makes us consciously aware
of our existence in this power.

We must all stand in strength
and not faint or falter
allowing the infinite power
to flow and transform.

I shall not deny God His victory
God shall not be denied.

June 11, 1998

The Miracle

Transformation
is the process
that takes place
within the heart.

The mind, ego, and emotions
rebel against the change
but the Spirit of God propels the growth.

Within the heart.

As the process continues
a maturity takes place
one by one
mind – ego– emotions
find their place.
The process advances.

Within the heart.

Finally,
there is God's Light
God's Spirit
God's Love
shining from the Heart.

July 20, 1998

On The Path Of His Love

Life
consuming His children
with the activities
of the world.
Pain, suffering, struggle,
sometimes forgetting the Light.
Sometimes forgetting His Power.
Sometimes forgetting Him.

The path
is ever illuminated
by the Love from His Heart
in the Light of His Being.

All one has to do
is remain on the path
and one will realize
that it is
the path of Love.

The path to His Heart.

September 10, 1998

The Silence

The silence
that lives within God
lives within us all.

Is the birthplace
of sound
of light
of movement
of life
of love
expressions of eternity
of God.

The good
that comes from the silence
is given rebirth
when we venture into the silence
that lives within God
that lives within us all.

October 23, 1998

In The Power Of His Love

In the Spirit of His Power
is where I long to live
is where I live
is where I will always live.

In the spirit of His Power
is where the goodness of His Love grows
it always has
it always will.

In the Spirit of His Power
is where all Truth reigns.

December 18, 1997

Peace – Be Still

The silence of
God's power in motion
moving in the stillness
of His eternal peace.

Touching
but yet, not touching
guiding
in a way that only God can.

In the silence
of the peace
that is God.

Peace – Be Still.

May 28, 1998

Touching The Wind

Touching the wind
with God's Love
that flows through the hearts of those
who open themselves
to His presence.

Reflection!
It causes a reflection
of itself
to appear in every portion
of one's life.

Transformation!
It transforms
completely
totally – unconditionally
and awakens
the Life of God
that lives within us all.

Touching the wind.

March 27, 1998

Spirit Filled

Standing
in the midst of God's Power
one learns to love
be love
and share in the love of God.

His spirit
wraps Himself
extends Himself
and expands Himself
through the lives
of those who know
and Love Him.

Spirit filled
the state of being
of God
in God
with God.

May 14, 1998

The Moment God Kissed The Wind

The moment God kissed the wind
the breath of His Life
soared throughout eternity.

Touching every part of His creation
it nourish, it consoled, it bathed
every living creature knew God's Love.

God teaches mankind
through His actions and His thoughts.
Perfect examples, multiplied.

We are a foolish lot.
Our way could never be the best way.
God is in control – always has been – always will be.

The moment God kissed the wind
the breath of His Life
soared throughout eternity
and changed everything
forever.

January 15, 1998

The Wisdom Of God's Love

The wisdom of God's Love
is found in the results
that come from
living in
and through it,
and what it brings into the lives
of those
who worship and adore Him.

Also
it is what it brings
into the surrounding world.

The wisdom of God's love.

April 30, 1998

His Power - Love

His Power shines forth
through His softness
and the gentle nature
of His touch.

Is the same
in the ever-present power
of life
as it lives through us all.

It's expressed
through the essence of creation
diversity and union
coexisting with perfection.

His Power – Love

June 5, 1998

God's Calling

God's calling
is a mission that whispers
in the hearts of many
but is answered by the lives of a few.

Why is it that the burden of many
seems to always rest
upon the shoulders of such a small number?

Israel
was a small nation
that was used by God
to deliver a message to the world.
The message was one of salvation.

Jesus,
the Son, stood alone
and died so that the salvation of all
could be achieved.

So, when you stand alone
seeking to bring the Love of God
into the lives of those around you,
and are met with resistance
and sometimes hostility,
realize that the burdens of many
shall always rest upon the shoulders of a few.

I don't know why God ordained such,
but He did.
As such, if we are to do His will
we should realize the burden
that we must carry.

But only
if we are to do His will

That's the reality
of God's calling.

March 19, 1998

God Speaks

God speaks
through the hearts
of those who love Him
and are willing
to carry out His will
in the lives of others.

We listen
those who are His children
to the sound of His Voice
as the whisper
resounds through our hearts
and guides our every action.

We respond
those who are His children
to the directions He gives
the power He shares
the magic He creates
in the love He gives to us
to give and give and give.

May 7, 1998

The Magic Of God's Love

The magic of God's Love
is seen in the miracle of creation.

Through the breath, a thought, a word,
there was light
which became life because it was always life
existing in a form beyond our comprehension.

God is Love and Love is God.
Is the bases of all things
and is the magic of all transformation.

The magic of God's Love
is the magic of all creation
is the power that unites the hearts of those
who can love all individuals
equally as they love themselves.

December 21, 1997

To The Surface

His Heart
opened
a bubble floated
to the surface
of the minds
of everyone
everywhere.

It popped!

Some notice
some didn't.
Some responded
others didn't.
Some didn't care!

There was a message
a powerfully, profound message
of life,
love,
healing,
and power.

Some responded
others didn't!

August 10, 1998

The Magic Of God's Smile

The magic of God's smile
gives radience to the world.
It warms
consoles
gives life.

It radiates goodness
that He seeks to give to all the world.
It shines
comforts
inspires.

The magic of God's Smile
gives radiance to the world.
It's the smile
that glows on the faces
of those who know God.

The magic of God's smile.

February 4, 1998

The Kiss Of God

I felt God's breath
against the side of my face
He opened my eyes
allowing me to realize
the goodness of the life He's given to me.

The touch of His presence
consoled my heart.
He spoke – I listen – I understood – I followed.

March 5, 1998

Resting

Resting in the presence of God
I feel the movement of His will
forming emotions
thoughts
desires
repulsions
inspirations
excitements.

Resting in the silence
reality rises
bringing certainty
to the things I must do.

June 2, 1998

Riding The Wings Of God

Riding the wings of God
is where I long to remain
free from the hardships
that life's conflicts create,
that people often face,
that challenges maintain.

Freedom to soar and touch,
to build and grow
to empower the empowered
to love and be loved
freely, unconditionally, eternally.

Riding the wings of God
causes one to flow into the depths of creation
but one learns the truth
about what makes God, God,
and leaves one with a sense of detachment
knowing that God is God
and therein lies one's freedom.

Riding the wings of God.

August 27, 1998

Dear Lord

People ask you
why and when,
in search of answers to their desires.
They don't realize
that the why and when
are not the questions that should be asked.

Your power is pure
and
your purpose complete.

Once a person accepts that reality,
the why and when
no longer exist,
and one learns to flow with the power
that you give to each.

Dear Lord, I thank you!

October 8, 1998

The Silence Of God's Voice

I sit
silence surrounds me
flows through me
becomes me
as I become silence.

The empty space
between thoughts
living there in peace
activity blossomed into creativity
creativity blossoms into life.

Life blossoms into God
in the beginning was the Word.
The Word was God
God was the silence.

April 16, 1998

Inner Peace — Outer Peace

The peace of God be with you!

Words echoing
in the chamber of my heart.
Peace
power
one and the same in the realm of the Spirit.

The kingdom of heaven
is within
is within
is within
but expresses itself
through the illusion of the world we see
every day of our lives.

But it all begins within
with the peace
which is the power
of God's love
channeled through the events
that are actions that manifest in our outer world,
as we think those things
as though they are.

Inner peace – outer power
the kingdom of heaven is within.

February 5, 1998

A Memory Of Transformation

The span of time
comes and goes
but
the memories of growth
remain ever present within our realms of thinking.

A memory of
meditation and prayer
when the Spirit was touched
and lives were changed.

That change
created a different view of reality
and
presented a different meaning to life.

It became permanent.

December 27, 1997

Wonderment

Winds flow from the deep
water moved through the sky
the ever present suns rays
pierced eternity.

Heartbeats inspire life
bloodflow purifies systems
lungs absorb elixirs
giving strength to His creation.

Creation in the garden of Eden
generations of fulfillment and purpose
miracles and continuous motion
lifelines from the unity of two.

Soft bubbles rising in His Heart
new worlds from every thought
understanding growing from compassion
the wonderment of Him creating it all.

May 20, 1998

Talk To Me, Lord

Allow me to hear the sound of your voice
in my heart – in your mind
where the peace of your love
becomes the peace of my love
and I fully understand the meaning
of your existence.

Your existence
lives within me in the form of Love
Your love that's within me
seeks expression in all others – in all things
in a pureness of creation,
your creation – which is perfect
because you are perfect
in love.

Allow me to hear the sound of your voice
in my heart – in your mind
where the peace of your love
becomes a peace of my love
and I fully understand the meaning
of your existence.

I love you, Lord!

March 11, 1998

When God Moved

When God moved
the beginning became the end
and the end, the beginning.

His first thought
laid the foundation
by writing the plan
for every single thing
that would come to pass.

When God moved
the freedom of choice was born
and humans realize the power.

The first actions
laid the foundation
by making the choices
to strip themselves
of the infinite power of creation.

When God moved
the beginning became the end
and the end, the beginning.

January 4, 1998

A Touch Of God's Love

A touch of God's love
is all that it takes
to transform the lives and events
that all people experience each day.
A touch of God's love
was all it took
to transform the universe
and create the experiences we all live through.

A touch of God's love
is the foundation
on which all life stands, lives, grows, and passes
away
only to transform and live on a higher plane.
All it takes is a touch
merely a tiny touch
of His love
to bring a smile to the face of a child
a tear to the eyes of happiness
and bubbles of joy from the hearts of good people.

A touch of God's love

March 16, 1998

A Special Moment With God

Silence
engulf the world
from within.

God moved upon the deep.

I sat.
I listened.
I learned.

Silence
flowed from the depths
of itself
carrying a simple message
from God.

It's found
in the silence
but is projected
in love.

I sat. I listened. I learned.

September 3, 1998

About the Author

G. Ashanti Witherspoon was raised in Chicago, Illinois, within a strong Episcopal family. Having been influenced by the streets, he ventured into a life of crime involving gangs and later another criminal organization. He left Chicago on the run from criminal charges in 1971. On January 17, 1972, following an armed robbery and shootout with the Shreveport (Louisiana) police, he was shot twice (once in the head and once through both legs). In November 1972, he was sentenced to 75 years without the benefit of parole, probation or suspension of sentence, in the Louisiana State Penitentiary in Angola, Louisiana.

He entered prison as an angry and violent young man. He later developed a mind shift when he accepted Christ back into his life. During the course of his confinement he was actively involved in a variety of educational and personal development programs. He began publishing a spiritual newsletter named Street Talk which was geared toward young people involved in crime. Some of his other activities include working as an Inmate Counsel Substitute (paralegal) in the prison's Legal Programs Department; HIV/AIDS Peer Educator (where he counsels all incoming prisoners), president of the CPR T.E.A.M. (where he instructed prisoners and people in society in C.P.R. and was one of the only three inmates in the country qualified to train instructors under the certification of *Instructor Trainer by the American Heart Association*), Toastmasters (public speaking), the Jaycees (speaking and community leadership development) and a member of the Full Gospel Businessmen's Fellowship, The Church of Transfiguration (Episcopal Prison Ministry) and Kairos Prison Ministry. He became a teacher, counselor, minister, speaker, leader and mentor to everyone around him; teaching numerous classes over the years that helped men develop as leaders and speakers. After twenty years the prison administration, under the approval of the Louisiana Department of Corrections, allowed him to travel throughout the state and give his testimony as a means to deter young people away from lives of crime and focus their lives on God. He was prominently featured in the award winning film, The Farm Life Inside Angola Prison (aired internationally and nominated for an Academy Award), in 1998.

Following a change in the law, he was presented before the Louisiana Parole Board and on June 18, 1999, was granted parole. Since that time he has been an associate pastor at Miracle Place Church, an international speaker, trainer and mentor, obtained his doctorate degree in Theology, teaches college courses with his wife Susan (at the Leaders Institute) and together they coordinate The Society of Servant Leaders, Inc. (www.societyofservantleaders.com) and a business The Withershine Group, LLC. He has a daughter (Bwashena who is working on a joint autobiography on their lives separated by prison bars) and three grandsons, and his wife Susan has a son and daughter. They love life and people and live by the philosophy that "Nothing Can Stop You, Except You."

www.ingramcontent.com/pod-product-compliance
Lightning Source LLC
Chambersburg PA
CBHW062055090426

42740CB00016B/3148